# FEATHER & BONE

*New Women's Voices Series, No. 165*

*poems by*

# Kathleen Williamson

*Finishing Line Press*
Georgetown, Kentucky

# FEATHER & BONE

Copyright © 2022 by Kathleen Williamson
ISBN 979-8-88838-041-3 First Edition
All rights reserved under International and Pan-American Copyright Conventions. No part of this book may be reproduced in any manner whatsoever without written permission from the publisher, except in the case of brief quotations embodied in critical articles and reviews.

## ACKNOWLEDGMENTS

Many thanks to the editors of the following journals in which these poems first appeared, sometimes in slightly different versions or with different titles.

*Lunate*: "Feather & Bone"
*Poetry International Online Quarterly*: "Rue"
*Newtown Literary*: "Pluck" and "Roost"
*Poetry Distillery*: "Hollow-Boned"
*Boston Literary Magazine*: "Solitary Migration"

Eternal gratitude to all who helped me with this collection, especially Jennifer Franklin, beloved teacher, who was with me from the beginning; Stacey Balkun at Poetry Barn who helped shape these poems into a manuscript; and Laura Desmarais who held my hand at the very end as we sweated through every detail.

Publisher: Leah Huete de Maines
Editor: Christen Kincaid
Cover Art: *Seacliff and Gulls* by Nishii Keigaku, photographed for Kagedo Japanese Art by Dick Busher, dickbusher.com
Author Photo: Lynda Shenkman
Cover Design: Elizabeth Maines McCleavy

Order online: www.finishinglinepress.com
also available on amazon.com

Author inquiries and mail orders:
Finishing Line Press
PO Box 1626
Georgetown, Kentucky 40324
USA

# Table of Contents

Feather & Bone ............................................................. 1

Grosbeak ...................................................................... 2

Clutch ........................................................................... 3

Brood ............................................................................ 4

Hatch ............................................................................ 5

Rue ................................................................................ 6

Nestling ........................................................................ 7

Coo ................................................................................ 8

Plunge ........................................................................... 9

Blur ............................................................................. 10

Devour ........................................................................ 11

Siren ............................................................................ 12

Nocturnal ................................................................... 13

Thump ........................................................................ 14

Caged .......................................................................... 15

Pluck ........................................................................... 16

Prey ............................................................................. 17

Roost ........................................................................... 18

Hollow-boned ............................................................ 19

Solitary Migration .................................................... 20

Murmuration ............................................................. 21

*To Eric, for his infinite patience and love*

## FEATHER & BONE

Shortly after sunrise
while the sky still holds roses

crows make their clamorous
commute to the river or the parkway

or wherever they go to eat the dead.
The helicopter hovers

over a home with a white
picket fence, quenched candle

in each window-boxed window.
I don't know how long it will loom.

The small boy and his younger sister
have already been bagged

and removed along with their parents
the murdered and the murderer.

Still the helicopter rends the sky.
Their teachers say the boy

was named for a poet,
the girl wore pigtails in her hair.

I was afraid the helicopter
would be here all morning but

it has withdrawn, quick as a knife.
By the parkway, the crows wait

for the circling vultures to land
and crack open the carcass.

## GROSBEAK
### *for Christian Cooper*

Your throat looks slit.
Breast the color

of blood just spilled.
We are in in The Ramble

in Central Park, where it once
was too dangerous to walk.

Your beak opens and emits
a squeak like sneakers

on a gym floor, as if scrambling
away from an assailant.

Morning illuminates you—
a contrast in black and white

written with ferocity.
Your call is a weep,

weep and I wonder if
your crimson chest

comes not from a cut throat
but from a heart that has burst.

## CLUTCH

Under the eaves of my porch
the robin makes a mess.
The steps are covered with twigs
and too much red ribbon.

Her nest is loose and sloppy
her alarm note a raucous cackle.
In a fever she abandons this nest
and builds on the garage—

her time must be near. But this space
is no better. The racket of the closing
door pushes her further and further
into madness.

I find two eggs,
Tiffany box blue,
cracked and pouring life
onto the driveway.

**BROOD**

My first worry,
when I wake,
is of you,
as is my last.
It is only by the sea, trying
and trying
to distinguish sanderling
from sandpiper—
or in the woods,
listening to the *white-throated
sparrow's five-note song,
pleading and pleading—*
it is only then that you—
and I— can disappear.
I live for long moments
not consumed by us.

## HATCH

Wind flies up, drags
dry leaves to clatter

on glass and rattles
the bath fan.

Remember the summer
starlings nested in that vent?

Their high sliding lament
and slurred whistles

lured us into madness.
When their young fledged,

we sealed the vent,
but the damage was done.

We found gashes in the duct
and feathers in the attic.

**RUE**

Her children venture into her darkened room, sit on the edge
of the bed, rest their bodies against the warmth of her thigh

and sometimes she'll tell them of their brother's tenth summer,
how she picked him up after an extra week at camp and found

him flitting in the woods, covered in mud, naked save a loin cloth
he'd fashioned with lanyard and what was left of his jeans.

Tufts of feathers and evergreen were tucked in his hair
and the last of his baby fat had melted away. He wolfed down

the cookies she'd brought, with neither a please nor a thank you.
Now, whenever she reminiscences about their brother,

dead more than a year, she never pictures the young man he had
grown into, but the way he looked that green and feathered summer.

## NESTLING

From the moment you jumped
from the cavity of the tree,
feather-light and bouncing,
you followed me.

I thought you precocial,
born with open eyes,
able to run and feed
yourself at once.

Little sparrow,
I was wrong.

You were born altricial.
You need the warmth
of all my brooding.

## COO

I have been told to mirror your feelings,
but how can I reflect your anger and despair?

Like lightning they will scorch you
 and the earth beneath your feet.

I want to offer you the softness
of my breast, carry your sorrow

on my back, so you can wander fields
of poppies, sleep when you are weary.

When rain comes,
let me absorb every drop.

**PLUNGE**

The bird | bright blue | big-headed
darted down the length of the lake

and you were off | down the path
gravel flying | your heels | striking
your bottom | never | taking your eye

off the bird | it landed on a branch
slung low | all its focus | on black water

it must have a nest | full of chicks
their begging | ringing | in its ears
their constant need | driving it

to keep bringing | and bringing
more | and more | and more

I did not know | then | how
hardwired | the urge | to feed is

The bird | gave a clattering
 rattle | dove headfirst
  | Certain

## BLUR

In warm summer rain
each humming bird

flutters, fanning
its tail in the sun shower.

Iridescent beings then
perch to preen—

intent on reflecting
the beauty of the sun.

My love, why do you hide
the shine of your body?

## DEVOUR

In the calm and shallow
a  heron walks in slow
motion, lifts one muddy foot
then the other.
Three black feathers at the back of its head stream in the wind.

Lulled by the sunshine of yesterday,
I'm unprepared.
Barefaced and gloveless,
my coat too thinly woven
to protect me.

                                              Still I watch.

The heron has found a bounty,
a life is pulled from the water
every few seconds,
flailing in the grip
of the mighty bill,
before being swallowed whole.
How long can each live
in its belly?

## SIREN

A mother of seven dies alone
a pint of pus pours from a young man's lungs

a man is found dead on the C train
and another on the 4 line.

And here in the heart of the worst
hit city in the nation

fish are spawning in the shallows of ponds
oak crown catkins team with warblers

yellow blue orange green
Before me - so close - a fire engine red

cardinal announces itself over and over—
*what cheer, what cheer, cheer, cheer, cheer*

drowning out every other siren in the city.

# NOCTURNAL

I am led right to him by the mob
dive-bombing the hemlock,
their frantic, throaty caws
recruit blue jays and more crows—
*the cold river of their hatred roils.*

After a night of cutting up his victims,
the owl opens one long-lashed yellow eye,
lazily closes it, opens the other, unruffled.
His talons grip the swaying
branch at the very center of the tree.

No other raptor holds me captive
like this. I arrive in day and stay
alone in the darkening wood.
By the time the owl calls no
light lingers here. I'm too afraid

to cross the field to my car, coyotes
and the men who live in nearby
trailers may intrude upon my path.
I kneel beneath the tree, find trophies
the owl has dropped from his throat.

Thumb-sized, bone-filled.

## THUMP

Smudge on window—
where you flung

your hungry body.
Was it a vain attempt

to escape pursuit,
or were you

rushing, rushing
to keep up, did you

close your eyes,
and fly headlong

toward the sun?
I hold your fluttering

body. Feel your heart
pulse in my hand.

## CAGED

I will bring you artisanal bread
with chèvre and mushrooms
and sneak in champagne
so you can hear the cork pop.

Scent of crisp autumn air
I will hide in my hair.
A chocolate cake I will bring
to you and when you slice it

the scent of honeysuckle
will waft into your cinder-block cell
and out will spill
the light of the Milky Way.

Over the clank of keys,
you will hear the wail
of a loon across black water.

## PLUCK

She's a little bit of a thing
but has substance and style
the way she twists
a black rag round her head
the way she lays open
the *New York Times*
on top of all her possessions
neatly folded in a shopping cart
the way she reads through
a magnifying glass
standing in a gutter
street jangling all around her
and she never flinching.

## PREY

I'm out of options, that's why I'm mounting the grimy
marble steps of the New York Public Library
past Fortitude, past Patience, into the once lofty lobby.

A librarian points me toward the Ladies, down
dim halls, missing half their bulbs, and then down
two flights into the building's very bowel.

A man steps from a shadow
follows me.

I race back to the safety of the librarian. Him?
she squints, That's just Harry. Perfectly harmless. Does it
all day, she says, every day. Follows women.
To the Ladies, I mean. Wouldn't hurt a dove.

Because I have to go, I retrace my steps, enter
the echoing restroom, Harry at the door. I let him
listen to me pee. We're both getting by in the hard city,
finding relief however we can.

## ROOST

Make the time, some time
to journey to the refuge
at Jamaica Bay.
Park your car and cross
the drag-raced boulevard.

Climb over a blown tire and
crunch through broken glass.
Follow the trampled path,
until the air grows closer
and mosquitos sing in your ear.

Go still. Go further. Choose
a blind on a swampy puddle.
See the tree slung low,
brimming with feathered bronze.

Remember their scarlet cousins,
flying by the thousands to roost
on mangroved island. Watch
the crescent moon slip into the bay.

Worship like an ancient Egyptian—
Bury them with your dead.

**HOLLOW-BONED**

Even the trudge
through mud
sucking at our soles
single file
in the predawn
downpour
                                  makes me happy.
At a stop in the line
                                in this perfect darkness
we bump into each other,
then grope our way
into the bird blind.
                              We've been told
to stay silent, but when black fades
to charcoal, Christine whispers that
the smudge on the ice is the cranes.
                                We've heard them all
along, of course, waking up,
their croaking a raucous purring.
The sky brightens to silver
                                and I can see a red crown
on the slender head
of each bustled gray body.
                                I wish they would dance,
but they are crowded
on this melting patch of ice
there is less ice this year
than last, which was less
than the year before.
They are hungry
to fly to the stubble
in the cornfields
                                I can hear it in their voices.

## SOLITARY MIGRATION
*for Bridget*

Long before sunrise
she is on her bike,
her legs like pistons
on the old post road.
She sought solitude
but now she feels it
in her throat—
tears blur her path.
To rally she sings
in the dark, an old
song about surrender.
Out of the woods,
as if summoned
by her song,
bounds an eight-point buck.
He gallops beside her.
Clipped to her bike,
she pedals faster,
the buck keeps pace.
She never thinks
to stop. Her voice
is silenced, the only
sound the clatter
of hooves on pavement.
Her breath beats
time with his.
She smells his musty,
mushroom scent,
feels the heat
of his body
sees her reflection
in his black eye.

## MURMURATION

I'm waist deep in the dark
green water, my back to

the high-rised and birdless shore,
training my eye on the horizon,

hoping for a pelican.

And the next wave is a silver wall
of fish swimming at me.

I dig my feet into the sand,
steady myself for the brunt

of fish, brace myself for their blunt
noses, I can see each round eye

blank and unwavering,

but just as I'm about to be hit
the school splits    and goes around

seals itself seamlessly together behind me.
I'm enveloped in fish for an hour,

reach out my hand, my foot, to touch
their energy—it would be like touching a star—

but they always evade me.

The ocean draws the warmth
from my bones, but I'll stay here

within the thumping heart of it all.

**NOTES:**

Italicized lines in "Brood" are from "North Haven" by Elizabeth Bishop

Italicized line in "Nocturnal" is from "In the Pinewoods, Crows and Owl" by Mary Oliver

**Kathleen Williamson's** poems have appeared in *Ponder Review, Newtown Literary, The Healing Muse,* as well as other literary journals. She is the winner of the *SLAB* Elizabeth R. Curry Poetry Contest for her poem, "To the Reader who Buys Every Fairy Tale," which was chosen to be part of the English curriculum at Grace Academy, Hartford, Connecticut. She is published in *Let Lightning Set Us on Fire*, a chapbook produced by Poetry Well to accompany its staging of love poems. Both the chapbook and the evening were named after the final line of her poem, "Porch in a Storm." As a winner in the *Poetry in the Pavement* project, she has a poem set in stone in Sleepy Hollow, New York.

She attended Bread Loaf Writers' Conference and studies at the Writing Institute at Sarah Lawrence College, Hudson Valley Writers' Center and The Writers Studio. She is on the Board of Saw Mill River Audubon and a Cofounder and Board Member of Films on Purpose, an organization that screens documentaries about social justice and the environment. She taught poetry classes on Zoom during the earliest, darkest days of the pandemic from her home in Pleasantville, New York.

www.ingramcontent.com/pod-product-compliance
Lightning Source LLC
Chambersburg PA
CBHW022128090426
42743CB00008B/1060